BASIC/NOT BORING
SCIENCE SKILLS

HUMAN BODY & HEALTH

Grades 4–5

Inventive Exercises to Sharpen
Skills and Raise Achievement

Series Concept & Development
by Imogene Forte & Marjorie Frank

Exercises by Marjorie Frank

Illustrations by Kathleen Bullock

Incentive Publications, Inc.
Nashville, Tennessee

About the cover:
Bound resist, or tie dye, is the most ancient known method of fabric surface design. The brilliance of the basic tie dye design on this cover reflects the possibilities that emerge from the mastery of basic skills.

Cover art by Mary Patricia Deprez, dba Tye Dye Mary®
Cover design by Marta Drayton and Joe Shibley
Edited by Charlotte Bosarge

ISBN 0-86530-587-0

PRINTED IN THE UNITED STATES OF AMERICA
www.incentivepublications.com

TABLE OF CONTENTS

CELEBRATE BASIC SCIENCE SKILLS

Basic does not mean boring! There certainly is nothing dull about . . .

  . . . solving mysteries about strange and curious body episodes

  . . . untangling mistaken identities of body parts

  . . . eavesdropping on cell phone conversations about body cells

  . . . learning the talents of the epiglottis, pancreas, patella, and parathyroids

  . . . reading X-rays to identify the bones that have been fractured

  . . . figuring out how patients taste and smell hospital food

  . . . searching for a swallowed tooth in someone's digestive system

  . . . sympathizing with 20 different complaining patients in the emergency room

The idea of celebrating the basics is just what it sounds like—enjoying and getting good at knowing the parts of the body and the way they function. Each page invites learners to try a high-interest, appealing exercise that will sharpen or review one specific science skill, concept, or process. This is no ordinary fill-in-the-blanks way to learn. These exercises are fun and surprising. Students will do the useful work of deepening science knowledge while they follow dozens of delightful patients, doctors, and workers around a medical clinic. These quirky characters will lead them to explore and deepen their understanding of the functioning of the body and the basics of health and fitness.

The pages in this book can be used in many ways:
- to sharpen or review a skill or concept with one student
- to reinforce the concept with a small or large group
- by students working independently
- by students working under the direction of a parent or teacher

Each page may be used to introduce a new skill, reinforce a skill, or assess a student's ability to perform a skill. There's more than just the great student activity pages. You will also find an appendix of resources for students and teachers—including a glossary of terms related to health and the human body, and a ready-to-use test for assessing science concepts and processes.

The pages are written with the assumption that an adult will be available to assist the student with his or her learning. It will be helpful for students to have access to science resources, textbooks, encyclopedias, library books, and Internet reference sources.

As your students take on the challenges of these adventures with the human body and health, they will grow. As you watch them check off the basic science skills they have sharpened and standards they have mastered, you can celebrate with them!

The Skills Test

Use the skills test beginning on page 56 as a pre-test and/or a post-test. This will help you check the students' mastery of the basic skills and understandings in the area of the human body and health. It can also help prepare them for further success on tests of standards, instructional goals, or other individual achievement.

SKILLS CHECKLIST FOR
HUMAN BODY & HEALTH, Grades 4-5

✔	SKILL	PAGE(S)
	Identify different body processes, activities, and parts	10–13
	Identify different body organs	12–13
	Distinguish between cells, tissues, organs, and systems; give examples of tissues, organs, and systems	14–15
	Identify different body systems and their functions	16–17
	Identify specific organs within systems	17
	Identify bones in the skeletal system and functioning of the skeletal system	18–19
	Identify function of teeth in the digestive process	20
	Identify joints, ligaments, cartilage and their functions	21
	Identify some muscles and understand the way muscles function	22–23
	Identify parts of the nervous system and understand the functioning of the system	24–27
	Show understanding of the function of sensory organs	28–31
	Identify the parts of the ear and the way they help in hearing	28
	Identify the parts of the eye and the way they help in seeing	29
	Show understanding of the way the nose and tongue work to enable the sensations of taste and smell	30
	Identify parts of the skin and show understanding of the functions of the skin	31
	Identify parts of the circulatory system and understand the functioning of the system	32–33
	Show understanding of the workings of the heart	32
	Identify parts of the respiratory system and understand the functioning of the system	34–35
	Identify parts of the digestive system and understand the functioning of the system	36–37
	Identify parts of the endocrine system and understand the functioning of the system	38
	Identify parts of the excretory system and understand the functioning of the system	39
	Show understanding of the purpose and functioning of the reproductive system	40–41
	Show understanding of the basic concepts of heredity and genetics	40–41
	Identify different diseases and disorders, their symptoms and causes	42–43
	Show understanding of the ways bodies can defend against disease, including natural defenses and other interventions	44–45
	Show understanding of nutrition concepts and components of a healthy diet	46–47
	Show understanding of the kinds of exercise and the way exercise is beneficial to health	48–49
	Show understanding of some basic first aid procedures	50–51
	Show ability to apply fitness and health concepts to personal life	52

HUMAN BODY & HEALTH

Skills Exercises

CURIOUS EPISODES

Some interesting occurrences are grabbing plenty of attention at Center City Health Clinic. Try to identify each of these curious episodes affecting patients or staff members.

1. Mr. Spoke has just hurried into the clinic with blood gushing from a cut on his forehead. After he arrives, some of the platelets in his blood begin to stick together near the surface of the cut and form a net-like substance. Other blood cells bunch up behind this "net." *What is happening?*

_____

2. Something has irritated the lining of Nurse Nadia's sinus passages. She tries to ignore it, but her body can't. Nerve endings in her nose are irritated and she suddenly (and quickly) expels air from her nose and mouth. A lot of other stuff (like dust, mucus, and moisture) is also expelled. *What has happened?*

_____

3. Dr. Femur is examining a patient in the emergency room. Dr. Femur has been at the hospital for 16 hours straight. Suddenly his brain has a desperate need for more oxygen. His body performs a reflex action that causes a quick intake of air. This forces oxygen into his lungs. *What is happening?*

_____

5. The patient in Room 25 is madly ringing the bell for a nurse. Some food from his tasty hospital lunch has gotten stuck in his trachea. He can't get any air into his lungs. *What is happening?*

_____

4. The patient in Room 115 has been swallowing air. Suddenly, some of the air escapes quickly from his stomach. It travels up through his esophagus and out through his mouth. This happens just as the night nurse comes in to take his temperature. He apologizes. *What has he just done?*

Use with page 11.

Name

10

6. The medical students are trying to listen to Dr. Radar's lesson on the appendix. One student is not paying attention because of a strange happening in her body. The nerve that controls her diaphragm has stimulated it, and her diaphragm is contracting without warning. This keeps happening over and over. It causes her to suck air in quickly. This makes her epiglottis snap shut suddenly, and causes an embarrassing noise. She can't seem to stop! *What is happening?*

10. Thousands of dead skin cells have mixed with the oils oozing from Dr. Danson's hair follicles. These dead skin cells have combined with dirt from the air to form a messy gunk. The flakes of this gunk are breaking off and falling on the shoulders of his jacket. *What is happening?*

7. The custodian is cleaning out Room 14 after a patient has gone home. He hurries out into the hall, his arms loaded with trash, and knocks over a cart filled with glasses, pitchers, and other containers. This causes a loud crash. A visitor is alarmed by the crashing noise behind her. A substance pours into her blood and prepares her for emergency action such as running away. *What is this substance?*

11. The receptionist on the overnight shift in the Emergency Room did not get enough sleep today. She's fallen asleep at her desk. Somehow the flow of air through the passages at the back of her mouth and nose are blocked. Structures in the back of her throat vibrate and rub against each other when she breathes. This makes an embarrassing sound, but she's asleep so she doesn't hear it! *What is happening?*

8. While a patient digests the macaroni and cheese she ate for dinner, her liver is smashing some substances into tiny pieces. *What is this substance?*

12. Belinda Blood is finished with her shift at the lab. She steps out the door to head for her car in the parking lot. It is cold and windy outside, and she doesn't have a coat. Her body gives a reflex response to the cold air. Her muscles begin to contract on their own. This produces heat and gives some warmth to her body. *What is happening?*

9. The new patient in Room 276 is experiencing a strange reaction happening inside her body. Her diaphragm muscle and the muscles in the wall of her abdomen are contracting strongly. This is forcing partly-digested food up and out of her stomach. *What is happening?*

Use with page 10.

Name

MISTAKEN IDENTITIES

Charlie is a student at the medical clinic. He's discovered a list of body parts and the jobs they do in the body. Something is wrong with this list. Every part seems to have been identified incorrectly. Write the true identity for each body part described.

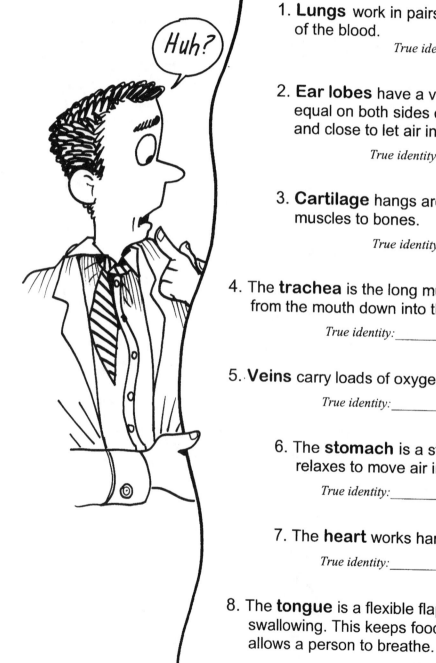

Huh?

1. **Lungs** work in pairs. They filter unwanted substances out of the blood.

   *True identity:*_____

2. **Ear lobes** have a very important job. They keep pressure equal on both sides of the eardrum. They are able to open and close to let air in and out.

   *True identity:*_____

3. **Cartilage** hangs around the muscles. It always joins muscles to bones.

   *True identity:*_____

4. The **trachea** is the long muscular tube that squeezes food from the mouth down into the stomach.

   *True identity:*_____

5. **Veins** carry loads of oxygen-rich blood away from the heart.

   *True identity:*_____

6. The **stomach** is a strong muscle that contracts and relaxes to move air in and out of the lungs.

   *True identity:*_____

7. The **heart** works hard to make blood cells.

   *True identity:*_____

8. The **tongue** is a flexible flap that covers the trachea during swallowing. This keeps food from getting into the airway that allows a person to breathe.

   *True identity:*_____

Use with page 13.

Name _____

12

This can't be right!

9. **Muscles** are spongy pads that are found between bones. They keep the bones from rubbing and grinding against each other.

    *True identity:*_____

10. The **spleen** hangs around at the end of the vertebrae column. This skinny bone is easy to bang if you sit down too hard.

    *True identity:*_____

11. The **colon** is an elastic bag that holds watery wastes filtered from blood by the kidneys. The waste collects until the bag gets close to full, then a muscle squeezes wastes out.

    *True identity:*_____

12. The **retina** is the outer layer of skin that protects the skin and body against germs. Besides being germproof, it is waterproof.

    *True identity:*_____

13. The **humerus** is the largest bone in the human body. It extends from the hip joint to the knee.

    *True identity:*_____

14. The **pupil** is the transparent window-like outer covering that protects the eye. Light passes through it into the eye.

    *True identity:*_____

15. **White blood cells** hold a substance called hemoglobin. Hemoglobin contains iron and is able to carry oxygen around the body.

    *True identity:*_____

16. The **epidermis** is the hard substance that covers the crown of a tooth. It protects the nerves and blood cells inside.

    *True identity:*_____

Use with page 12.

Name _____

CELL TALK

Some students are talking over their cell phones to review information for a test on body cells, tissues, and organs. There's a lot of static on all their phones, so they are having a hard time hearing well.

Here is what the students heard on each of 9 topics. Who is hearing the information correctly? For A–J, circle one or more names to show which students are hearing the correct information.

A. *Lexi hears*: The body is made up of about 50 million cells.
   Max hears: The body is made up of about 50 billion cells.
   Rex hears: The body is made up of about 50 thousand cells.
   Roxie hears: Billionaires have more cells than millionaires.

B. *Lexi hears*: Most cells last for the lifetime of the body.
   Max hears: Nerve cells should last a lifetime and cannot be replaced.
   Rex hears: Many cells have a limited lifetime, so the body must repair or replace them.
   Roxie hears: Cell phones last for the lifetime of the owner.

C. *Lexi hears*: Groups of different kinds of cells form tissues.
   Max hears: Groups of the same kinds of cells form organs.
   Rex hears: Groups of the same kinds of cells form tissues.
   Roxie hears: A lot of tissues are used in a jail cell.

D. *Lexi hears*: Cells reproduce by dividing.
   Max hears: Cells cannot reproduce.
   Rex hears: Cells reproduce by growing new parts that break off.
   Roxie hears: Cell phones have been known to reproduce.

E. *Lexi hears*: All cells need food, oxygen, and sunshine to stay alive.
   Max hears: All cells need food; only blood cells need oxygen.
   Rex hears: All cells need food and oxygen to stay alive.
   Roxie hears: All cells need oxygen, chocolate, and music to stay alive.

F. *Lexi hears*: Every organ in the body has a special job to do.
   Max hears: Eyes, ears, skin, and kidneys are examples of organs.
   Rex hears: Different kinds of tissues group together to form organs.
   Roxie hears: You cannot play a pipe organ if you have any missing organs.

Use with page 15.

Name

G. *Lexi hears:* The nucleus is the director of activity in each cell.

  Max hears: The cell membrane lets substances in and out of the cell.

  Rex hears: The mitochondria let substances in and out of the cell.

  Roxie hears: The ribosomes in the cell cause people to crave ripe fruit.

H. *Lexi hears:* Genes are carried only by cells in the reproductive system.

  Max hears: Every cell contains genes that give unique characteristics to the person.

  Rex hears: Genes are found only in brain cells.

  Roxie hears: Only people who wear jeans have genes in their cells.

I. *Lexi hears:* Cells form tissues, tissues form organs, and organs form systems.

  Max hears: All systems make use of the same organs.

  Rex hears: Blood is important for all body systems.

  Roxie hears: Cell phones make use of the body's nervous system.

Before they could finish their review, the students lost their cell phone connections. Finish the review for them.

J. Name the four different kinds of body tissue.

1. *connective*　　　3. _____

2. *epithelial (skin)*　　4. _____

K. Name 6 human body organs.

1. _____　　4. _____

2. _____　　5. _____

3. _____　　6. _____

L. Name 3 human body systems.

1. _____

2. _____

3. _____

Use with page 14.

Name

A SYSTEM FOR SYSTEMS

Different doctors at the clinic have different specialties. This means that different doctors know about and treat the different body systems. The clinic has a filing system for keeping track of patients having problems with different systems. The patient's file is placed with the doctor whose specialty matches the problem.

Read the names of the doctors and body systems. Then read the descriptions of the body systems (A-J). Write the name of the doctor who would work with the system described.

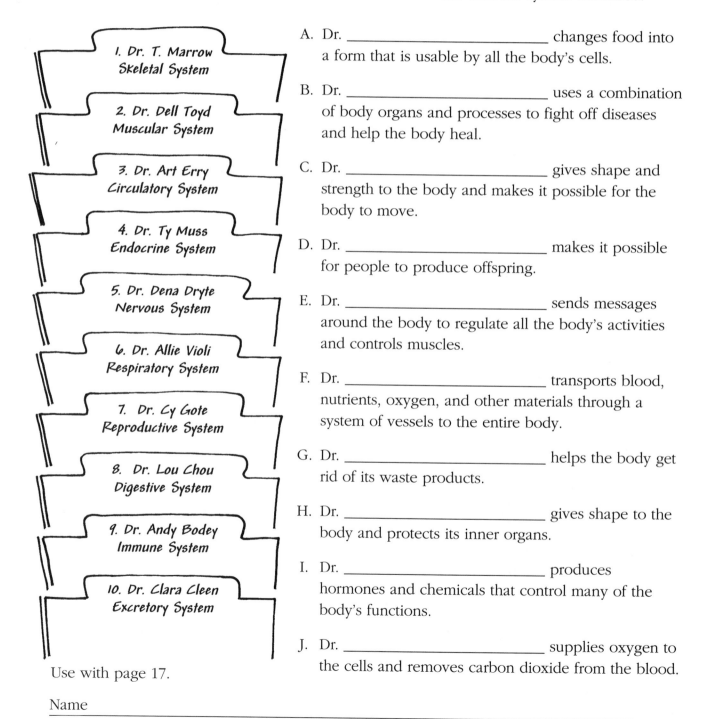

1. Dr. T. Marrow
Skeletal System

2. Dr. Dell Toyd
Muscular System

3. Dr. Art Erry
Circulatory System

4. Dr. Ty Muss
Endocrine System

5. Dr. Dena Dryte
Nervous System

6. Dr. Allie Violi
Respiratory System

7. Dr. Cy Gote
Reproductive System

8. Dr. Lou Chou
Digestive System

9. Dr. Andy Bodey
Immune System

10. Dr. Clara Cleen
Excretory System

A. Dr. _____ changes food into a form that is usable by all the body's cells.

B. Dr. _____ uses a combination of body organs and processes to fight off diseases and help the body heal.

C. Dr. _____ gives shape and strength to the body and makes it possible for the body to move.

D. Dr. _____ makes it possible for people to produce offspring.

E. Dr. _____ sends messages around the body to regulate all the body's activities and controls muscles.

F. Dr. _____ transports blood, nutrients, oxygen, and other materials through a system of vessels to the entire body.

G. Dr. _____ helps the body get rid of its waste products.

H. Dr. _____ gives shape to the body and protects its inner organs.

I. Dr. _____ produces hormones and chemicals that control many of the body's functions.

J. Dr. _____ supplies oxygen to the cells and removes carbon dioxide from the blood.

Use with page 17.

Name

When a patient comes into the clinic with a problem, one of the nurses has to decide where to send her or him to get the best care. The nurse listens to the patient's symptoms and chooses a doctor. Which doctor would be a good one for each patient? Circle the best choice.

#1: Problem: thyroid gland
a. Dr. Chou
b. Dr. Cleen
c. Dr. Muss

#2: Problem: sternum
a. Dr. Gote
b. Dr. Marrow
c. Dr. Violi

#3: Problem: capillaries
a. Dr. Erry
b. Dr. Dryte
c. Dr. Bodey

#4: Problem: uterus
a. Dr. Dryte
b. Dr. Toyd
c. Dr. Gote

#5: Problem: small intestine
a. Dr. Violi
b. Dr. Chou
c. Dr. Erry

#6: Problem: diaphragm
a. Dr. Muss
b. Dr. Marrow
c. Dr. Violi

#7: Problem: neurons
a. Dr. Erry
b. Dr. Dryte
c. Dr. Cleen

#8: Problem: white blood cells
a. Dr. Bodey
b. Dr. Chou
c. Dr. Gote

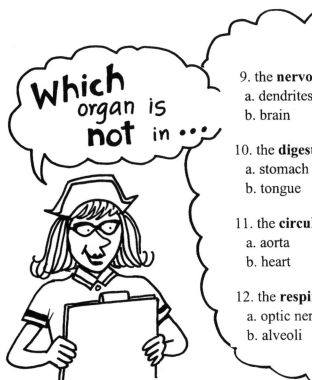

9 – 15: Circle one correct answer.

Which organ is not in ...

9. the **nervous system**?
a. dendrites   c. spinal cord
b. brain   d. spleen

10. the **digestive system**?
a. stomach   c. trachea
b. tongue   d. salivary glands

11. the **circulatory system**?
a. aorta   c. veins
b. heart   d. scapula

12. the **respiratory system**?
a. optic nerve   c. lungs.
b. alveoli   d. bronchi

13. the **muscular system**?
a. canines   c. deltoids
b. triceps   d. hamstrings

14. the **skeletal system**?
a. radius   c. atrium
b. fibula   d. clavicle

15. the **excretory system**?
a. tonsils   c. skin
b. kidneys   d. ureters

Use with page 16.

Name

BONES ON DISPLAY

In the X-ray lab, Dr. Marrow is looking at 10 X-rays of broken bones. He's explaining the different fractures to his students.

Look at each X-ray, and read the description of the bone. Then write the number of the bone (from the skeleton) and the name of the bone at the top of the X-ray.

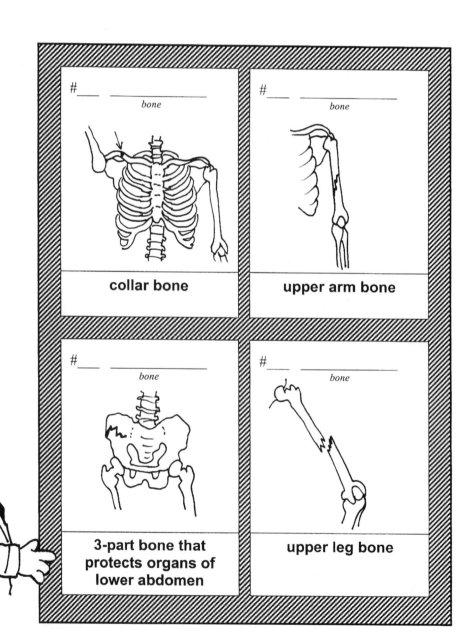

#_____ _____
bone

collar bone

#_____ _____
bone

upper arm bone

#_____ _____
bone

3-part bone that protects organs of lower abdomen

#_____ _____
bone

upper leg bone

Use with page 19.

Name

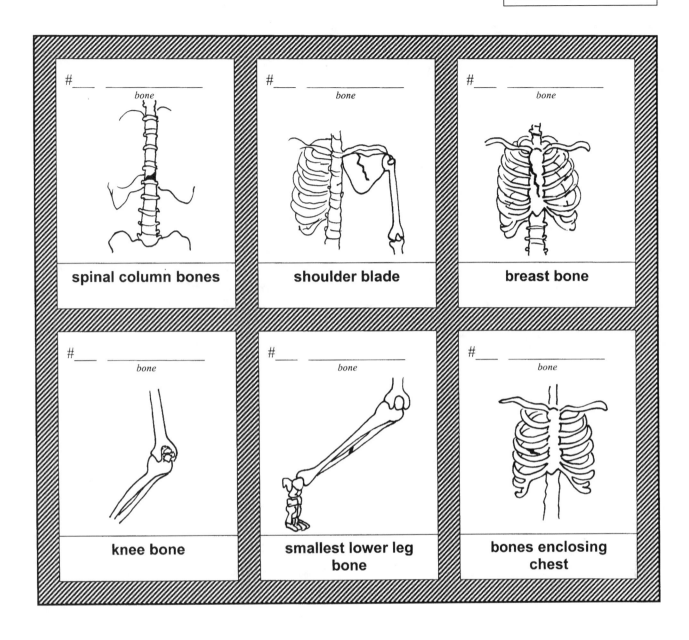

#___ _____
bone

spinal column bones

#___ _____
bone

shoulder blade

#___ _____
bone

breast bone

#___ _____
bone

knee bone

#___ _____
bone

smallest lower leg bone

#___ _____
bone

bones enclosing chest

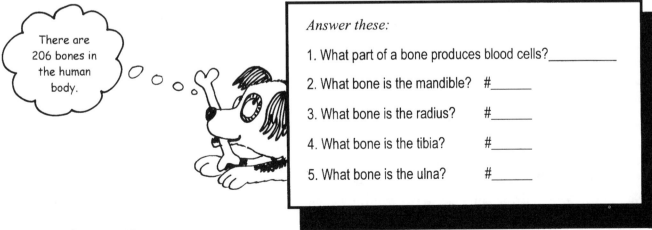

There are 206 bones in the human body.

Answer these:

1. What part of a bone produces blood cells?_____

2. What bone is the mandible?   #_____

3. What bone is the radius?   #_____

4. What bone is the tibia?   #_____

5. What bone is the ulna?   #_____

Use with page 18.

Name

CUT & GRIND, TEAR & MASH

In the middle of an operation, surgeon Dr. Deena Dryte got a toothache so terrible that she could not continue. She turned the surgery over to her assistant and headed straight for the dentist.

Fill in the missing words in the information about Dr. Dryte's teeth and her visit to the dentist. Label A-E on the diagram with their correct labels (pulp, dentin, enamel, root, crown).

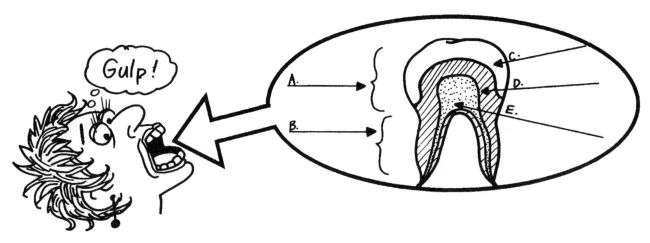

The dentist took a careful look inside Deena's mouth. Ordinarily, she's glad she has teeth. Today, she's not so sure, since she is in terrible pain. Her teeth are of four different kinds. The eight center front teeth *(4 on top, 4 on bottom)* have sharp edges that can grab and cut food. These are her [1]_____. Next over are four slightly pointed _____ teeth *(2 on top, 2 on the bottom)*. These teeth can tear and bite hard food. Further back are eight [3]_____ *(4 on top, 4 on the bottom)* that crush food.

The tooth that is bothering Dr. Dryte today is the fourth kind of tooth. It is one of eight flat teeth at the back of her mouth *(4 on top, 4 on bottom)*. It is a [4]_____, one of the teeth that can grind and mash food. The dentist takes a close look at the tooth that is causing the pain. He examines the part of the tooth that is showing above the gum line. This is called the [5]_____. He sees a large area of decay, called a [6]_____. After giving her some medicine to numb the area, the dentist begins to drill through the [7]_____, which is the hard covering on the tooth. The decay has reached into the next layer, called the [8]_____. It has even decayed into the third layer, the [9]_____. This is the softest layer. It contains nerves and [10]_____ that nourish the tooth.

Dr. Dryte ignored her dental care too long. Now, she has a bad infection in the nerves of this tooth. The dentist will have to remove the nerves and fill the root of the tooth with steel. He won't have to pull the tooth, but it will be dead.

Name

TWIST, BEND & SWIVEL

Nurse Martin Meds must do plenty of twisting, reaching, bending, and swiveling during a day at work. He could not do all these movements if he didn't have certain structures in his body called joints. Answer these questions about the movements that are a part of his day.

1. _____ What kind of joint allows Nurse Meds to bend his knees to pick up a dropped needle?

2. _____ What kind of joint allows him to reach his arm above his head to clip an X-ray on the wall?

3. _____ What kind of joint allows him to bend his spine to make a bed?

4. _____ What kind of joint allows him to flip his hands over to carry a tray of medicine bottles?

5. _____ Which joint in his body makes it possible for him to bend his arm to lift up a patient?

6. _____ Which joints in his body make it possible for him to run down a hall to get to a patient's room quickly?

7. _____ What holds bones together at joints?

8. _____ What spongy substance keeps bones from grinding against each other where they touch?

Look at these examples of different kinds of joints.
Label each joint with the correct label: *hinge, pivot, ball & socket, or gliding*.

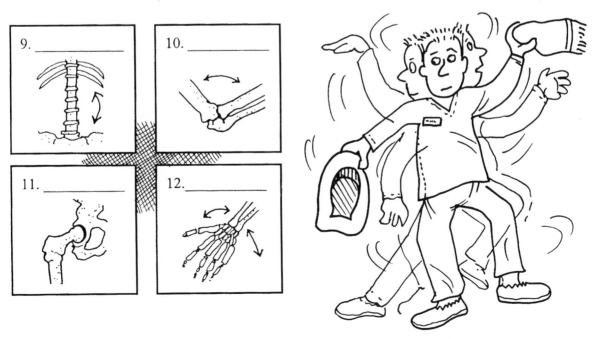

9. _____

10. _____

11. _____

12. _____

Name _____

YOU CAN'T MOVE WITHOUT THEM

Strong, flexible muscles are a must for nurse Sabrina. She needs strength to carry equipment, and to lift and move patients. So she stops in at the clinic's Fitness Center several times a weak to keep her muscles in good shape. Answer these questions about muscles and Sabrina's workout.

1. Which muscle is contracted when she lifts the weight towards her shoulder?

_____

2. Which muscle is relaxed?

_____

3. Which muscle is contracted when she lowers her arm back down?

_____

4. Which muscle is relaxed?

_____

5. Sabrina's thigh muscle bulges when she pushes weights with her feet. Are these muscles contracting or relaxing? _____

6. What kind of exercise should Sabrina do to increase the flexibility in her muscles? _____

7. Which is true about Sabrina's muscles? (Circle one or more.)
   a. Her muscles have more power when they are relaxed.
   b. Her muscles have more power when they are contracted.
   c. Her muscles can only pull.
   d. Her muscles can only push.

Use with page 23.

Name

8–12: Circle one or more correct answers.

8. Which is true about Sabrina's muscles?
   a. Her muscle tissue is made of muscle cells.
   b. Her leg muscles are involuntary muscles.
   c. Her triceps and biceps muscles are found in her arms.
   d. Her hamstrings and quadriceps muscles are in her legs.

9. The strong bands of tissue that connect her muscles to her bones are
   a. cartilage.
   b. nerves.
   c. tendons.
   d. ligaments.

10. The muscles that are connected to Sabrina's bones (her skeletal muscles) are
   a. smooth muscles.
   b. striated muscles.
   c. voluntary muscles.
   d. automatic (involuntary) muscles.

11. Sabrina's heart muscle is
   a. cardiac muscle.
   b. striated muscle.
   c. an automatic (involuntary) muscle.
   d. a voluntary muscle.

12. Smooth muscle can be found in the
   a. lining of Sabrina's blood vessels.
   b. leg muscles.
   c. lining of Sabrina's mouth.
   d. lining of Sabrina's intestines.

Use with page 22.

Name _____

THE GREAT COMMUNICATOR

Dr. Axon is describing the wonders of the brain to his students. She's using Zeke as a model to help describe some facts about how the brain and nervous system work. The students are asking many questions about Zeke's brain.

How will she answer these questions? Write the answer she might give to each one.

1. _____ 7. _____

2. _____ _____

3. _____ 8. _____

4. _____ _____

5. _____ 9. _____

6. _____ 10. _____

1. Which part of the brain helps Zeke keep his balance on a narrow bridge?

2. Which part of Zeke's brain helps him think up a new idea?

3. Which part of Zeke's brain helps him see, hear, smell, taste, and feel hot or cold?

4. Which part of Zeke's brain controls his breathing and his heartbeat?

5. Which part of Zeke's brain helps him work his arms and legs together to play basketball?

6. Which part of his nervous system relays messages between the brain and the rest of his body?

7. How is his central nervous system different from his peripheral nervous system?

8. What is the job of his motor neurons?

9. What is the job of his sensory neurons?

10. What is the job of his connector neurons?

Use with page 25.

Name

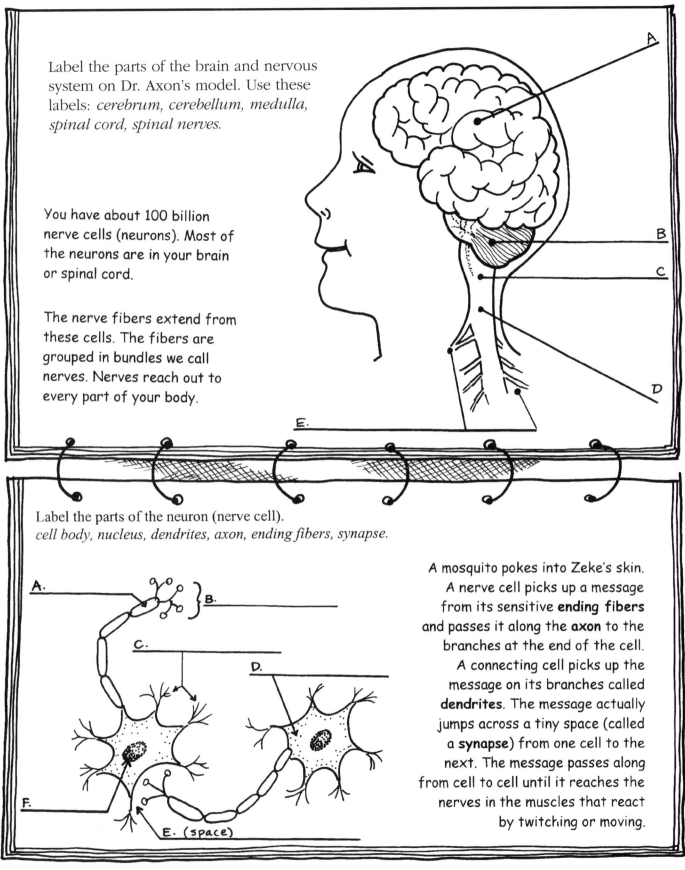

Label the parts of the brain and nervous system on Dr. Axon's model. Use these labels: *cerebrum, cerebellum, medulla, spinal cord, spinal nerves.*

You have about 100 billion nerve cells (neurons). Most of the neurons are in your brain or spinal cord.

The nerve fibers extend from these cells. The fibers are grouped in bundles we call nerves. Nerves reach out to every part of your body.

A _____

B _____

C _____

D _____

E. _____

Label the parts of the neuron (nerve cell).
cell body, nucleus, dendrites, axon, ending fibers, synapse.

A. _____

B. _____

C. _____

D. _____

E. (space) _____

F. _____

A mosquito pokes into Zeke's skin. A nerve cell picks up a message from its sensitive **ending fibers** and passes it along the **axon** to the branches at the end of the cell. A connecting cell picks up the message on its branches called **dendrites**. The message actually jumps across a tiny space (called a **synapse**) from one cell to the next. The message passes along from cell to cell until it reaches the nerves in the muscles that react by twitching or moving.

Use with page 24.

Name

BACKWARDS BRAIN TEASER

Brain and nerve specialist, Dr. Erv Nerve, has given his students a challenging puzzle about the nervous system. You will notice that the puzzle is already solved. But the clues to solve it are missing! Use the spaces on page 27 to write a clear clue for each word from the puzzle.

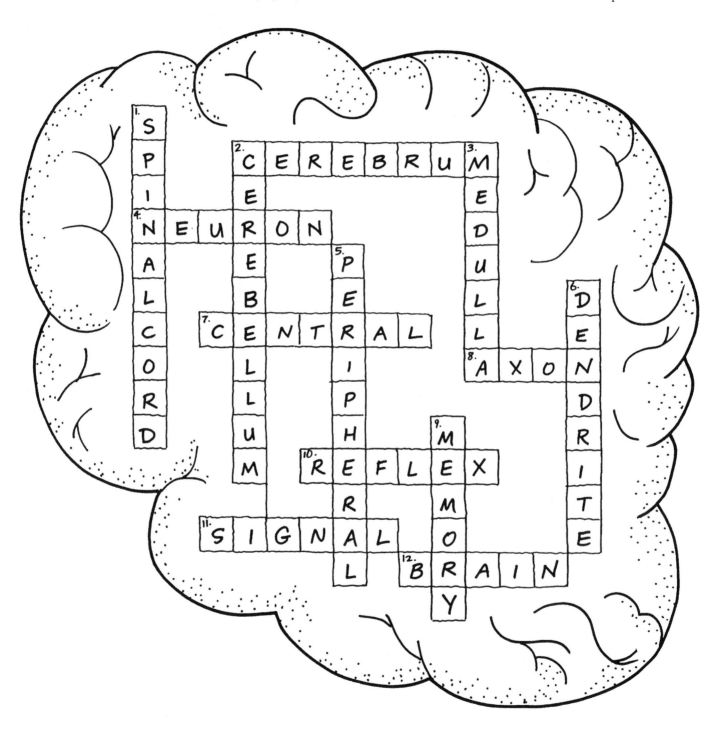

Use with page 27.

Name

Write a clear clue for each word in the puzzle.

PUZZLE CLUES

Across

2. _____

4. _____

7. *The part of the nervous system that*

8. _____

10. _____

11. _____

12. _____

Down

1. _____

2. _____

3. _____

5. *The part of the nervous system that*

6. _____

9. _____

Use with page 26.

Name _____

SOME SOUND STRUCTURES

Surgeon Susannah Slauter always listens to music before she operates because it keeps her from being tense. Today she's listening to a mixture of her favorite jazz, hip-hop, country, and pop music on her CD player.

Identify the parts of Dr. Slauter's ears that make it possible for her to enjoy this music. Write the name of the structure to match each letter and description.

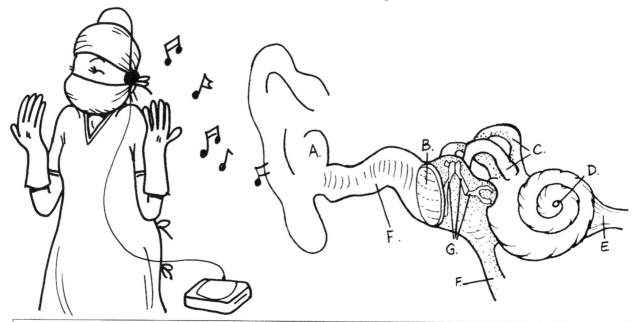

	What is the structure?
1. This stretched membrane separates her outer ear from her inner ear. It vibrates when the sound of the music hits it and passes the sound into the inner ear. (B)	
2. This coiled tube is filled with fluid. It also contains tiny hairs with nerve endings that pick up vibrations from the sound. The fluid vibrates from the sound and causes the hair cells to vibrate. The nerve endings vibrate and pass a signal on to the nerve that carries messages on to the brain. (D)	
3. This structure is shaped like a funnel. It catches sounds and directs them into Susannah's ear. (A)	
4. These canals contain fluid and nerve cells. The nerve cells are very sensitive to movement. They help Susannah keep her balance. (C)	
5. This tube is lined with hairs and produces wax. The sound waves carrying the music pass through this tube toward the eardrum. (F)	
6. These tiny bones pass the music vibrations from the eardrum on to her inner ear. *(Name all three bones.)* (G)	
7. This carries the music messages to her brain from cells in the coiled tube. (E)	

Name

A RARE SIGHTING

Chester Fryte has come racing to the Eye Clinic. He's seen a rare and scary sight: a strange monster-like shape in his bedroom. He knows that there can't be a huge hairy monster in his bedroom, so he thinks there must be something terribly wrong with his eyes.

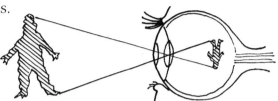

The doctor found nothing wrong with Chester's eyes. How did Chester see a monster? Fill in the missing information in the explanation.

Here's what happened, Chester: You left your big dark coat hanging over that tall, standing fan. Later, you woke up in a dark room. The shadow of the coat and fan reflected onto the wall. The shadow was even bigger than the real items—so big that it looked like a monster!

A. The light in the room reflected off the wall around the shadow. That light traveled through the thin, protective layer of your eye, called the _____ .

B. A small hole in the center of your eye, your _____ , let the reflected light pass into your eye. A muscle, the _____ , controls the size of that hole. (This muscle also gives color to your eye.)

C. The light still carried the image of the monster. It passed into the eye and through the _____ , a transparent disc that focuses light in your eye. This structure bent the light and turned the image of the monster upside-down.

D. The light with the image then shined onto an area in the back of the eye called the _____. It has millions of cells on it that are sensitive to light and color.

E. A structure sent the signals about the image from the back of your eye on to your brain. This structure is your _____.

The image did not stay upside-down or you would have seen the monster upside-down! Your brain is so smart that it turned the image right-side up. This is how that dark coat turned into a monster. When you go home, take a careful look in your bedroom, and you will see that there is no monster. No, there is nothing wrong with your eyes.

Name _____

 Basic Skills/Human Body & Health 4-5

COMPLAINTS TO THE COOK

Max has been in a hospital bed at the clinic for 36 days with badly battered tissues, broken bones, and hundreds of stitches. This means that he has eaten over 100 hospital meals. He has complained about most of them. He's complained about the appearance of the food. He's complained about the smell. And, mostly, he's complained about the taste.

Answer the questions about Max's experiences with his senses of taste and smell.

1. Max has some special cells that are sensitive to odors. What are these called?

_____

2. What do those cells do with the information about smell?

_____

There are over 3000 different smells that the human body interprets.

Yuck!

3. How does the scent of the food get into his nasal passages?

_____

4. For a week Max had a bad cold. He couldn't taste the food very well during that week. Why not?

_____

_____

5. In order for Max to taste, what substance in his mouth must first dissolve the food?

_____

6. What structures in his mouth allow him to taste tonight's macaroni and cheese?

_____

7. What part of his tongue tastes the sour lemonade? *(The cook forgot the sugar again.)*

_____

8. What part of his tongue tastes the extra sweet cherry pie? *(The cook put too much sugar in this.)*_____

9. What part of his tongue tastes the bitter artichoke-vinegar soup? *(This is the cook's specialty!)*_____

10. What part of his tongue tastes the salty spinach gumbo? *(The cook dumped the whole salt shaker in it!)*_____

Name _____

THE SKIN YOU'RE IN

Allie's letter is all about her skin. Some words that explain the functions and characteristics of the skin are missing. Write the missing words in the blanks.

Dear Yolanda,

I know I should be thankful for my skin. It holds my whole body together and keeps out [1] _____ and [2] _____. It also keeps my body temperature controlled by letting sweat evaporate through the [3] _____. Besides that, my skin allows me to feel things. It has specialized nerve endings that are sensitive to four things: [4] _____, [5] _____ [6] _____, and [7] _____.

But right now, my skin is driving me crazy. I came home from the camping trip last weekend with chapped lips, blistered feet, mosquito bites, and poison oak. My top layer of skin (the [8] _____), is infected and blistered. I know the nerve endings in my [9] _____ (the second layer), are irritated, because I am itching like mad! The nerves are sending itching and pain messages along to my [10] _____.

There's more! I am so sunburned! My skin was exposed to more of the sun's ultraviolet rays than the [11] _____ in my skin's pigment could handle. I know sunshine is good for me. It helps my skin make [12] _____ that my body needs. But I am miserable!

Your sore, itching, blistered friend,

Allie

Name _____

BLOOD ON THE MOVE

Erma Globin is nervous about having her physical exam today. At the beginning of the exam, Dr. Abe Orta feels her pulse and listens to her heart.

1. What causes Erma's pulse? _____

2. Where is a good place to feel her pulse? _____

3. Dr. Orta tells Erma that her heart rate is 75 bpm. What does this mean? _____

4. What causes the sound of Erma's heartbeat? _____

Look at the heart diagram. Write the number from the diagram to show the area of the heart being described. (Look at the words in bold print. Find the number that matches that part or area.)

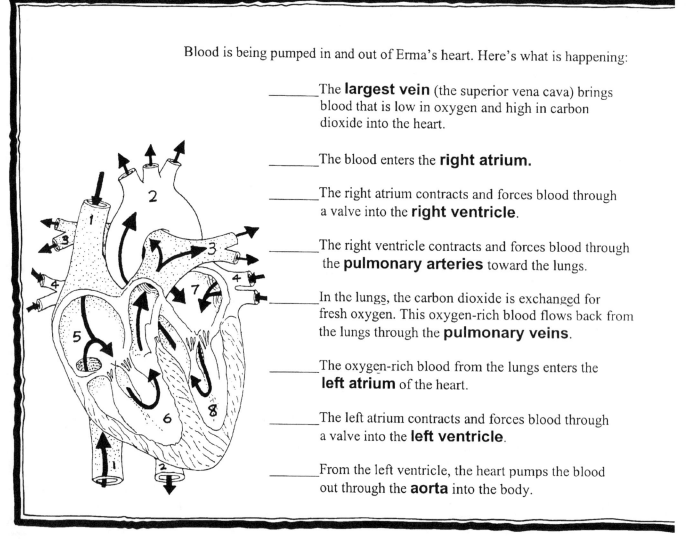

Blood is being pumped in and out of Erma's heart. Here's what is happening:

_____ The **largest vein** (the superior vena cava) brings blood that is low in oxygen and high in carbon dioxide into the heart.

_____ The blood enters the **right atrium.**

_____ The right atrium contracts and forces blood through a valve into the **right ventricle**.

_____ The right ventricle contracts and forces blood through the **pulmonary arteries** toward the lungs.

_____ In the lungs, the carbon dioxide is exchanged for fresh oxygen. This oxygen-rich blood flows back from the lungs through the **pulmonary veins**.

_____ The oxygen-rich blood from the lungs enters the **left atrium** of the heart.

_____ The left atrium contracts and forces blood through a valve into the **left ventricle**.

_____ From the left ventricle, the heart pumps the blood out through the **aorta** into the body.

Use with page 33.

Name

At the end of her physical exam, the doctor sends Erma for some blood tests. She waits nervously for her turn to get the needle put into her arm.

The receptionist in the lab offers her something to occupy her mind while she's waiting. It's a short test about blood. Erma is sure she can answer all the questions correctly.

How did she do? Read her answers. Circle the numbers of the questions she answered correctly.

What Do You Know About Your Blood?

Circle one of the choices for words to complete the sentence.

1. The disease fighters that make antibodies are the (**white blood cells, red blood cells**).

2. (**Plasma, Marrow**) is the part of blood that carries your digested food and waste products.

3. It is the (**protein, fat, hemoglobin**) in the blood cells that enables them to carry oxygen.

4. Your (**veins, arteries**) have valves to prevent the blood from flowing backwards.

5. The parts of your blood that helps your blood clot are the (**platelets, plasma**).

6. (**Veins, Arteries**) are blood vessels that carry blood away from the heart.

7. Blood travels around your body in tubes called (**vessels, axons, bronchi**).

8. Your (**red blood cells, white blood cells**) are the ones that carry oxygen.

9. Your (**veins, arteries**) are blue because they carry blood with wastes.

10. Your blood has many more (**red than white, white than red**) cells.

11. Blood flows at a higher pressure in your (**veins, arteries**).

12. The main vein in your body is the (**aorta, vena cava**).

13. The tiniest blood vessels are (**dendrites, capillaries**).

14. The aorta carries blood from the (**brain, heart, feet**).

15. The heart muscle is (**voluntary, involuntary**) muscle.

16. Your (**veins, arteries**) have the thickest walls.

Use with page 32.

Name _____

TAKE A DEEP BREATH

Kids from the Fourth Avenue Pre-School have come in for their vaccinations. Their respiratory systems are getting quite a workout, because there is a lot of screaming, gasping, and squealing. To make all this noise, they must do plenty of inhaling and exhaling of air.

Label the structures being used for all this breathing!

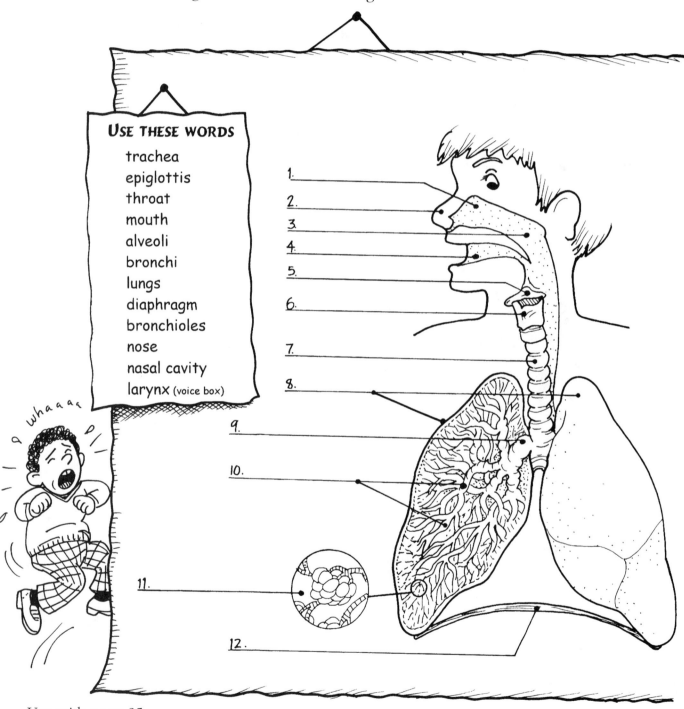

USE THESE WORDS

- trachea
- epiglottis
- throat
- mouth
- alveoli
- bronchi
- lungs
- diaphragm
- bronchioles
- nose
- nasal cavity
- larynx (voice box)

1. _____
2. _____
3. _____
4. _____
5. _____
6. _____
7. _____
8. _____
9. _____
10. _____
11. _____
12. _____

Use with page 35.

Name

Sam is breathing in and out rapidly as he worries about getting his shot. Answer these questions about how his respiratory system is working.

BREATHING IN

1. Where does air travel after it is taken into Sam's mouth?_____

_____

2. What happens to his ribs when he inhales?_____

3. What happens to his diaphragm when he inhales?_____

4. What happens to his epiglottis when he inhales?_____

5. What important substance is in the air he inhales?_____

6. What is the purpose of the hairs and mucus in his nose?_____

BREATHING OUT

7. What path does the air follow to leave her body?_____

_____

8. What waste substance is in the air that she exhales?_____

9. What happens to her ribs when she exhales?_____

10. What happens to her diaphragm when she exhales?_____

The best way to prevent choking is to keep food out of your mouth when you are laughing or talking.

On the average, you inhale and exhale more than 2000 times a day.

Use with page 34.

Name _____

FOLLOW WHAT WAS SWALLOWED

Oh, no! The dentist pulled Bert's tooth and dropped it in his mouth. Before the dentist could grab it, Bert swallowed it! At the clinic, the doctors are looking the X-rays and discussing the location of the tooth. Where will they find the tooth?

In each quote, name the part of the digestive system that they are discussing.

1. It has obviously moved beyond the muscular tube that squeezes food along toward the stomach.
What is the part?

_____

2. I don't see it anywhere in the neighborhood of the organ that makes bile to break up the fats in food.
What is the part?

_____

3. I see what looks like frogs' legs in this stretchy organ where food is churned around and acid pours in to digest proteins. But I don't see a tooth!
What is the part?

_____

4. Did anyone check to see if it is caught under the organ whose powerful muscles move food to the back of the throat?
What is the part?

_____

5. It's not near the organ that stores bile until it is needed for digestion.
What is the part?

_____

6. Is that a safety pin being squeezed along near the end of the digestive system to the place where water is removed from the solid wastes?
What is the part?

_____

7. Ahh! There it is! It has traveled all the way into the long, windy structure where food is in a form that it can pass through the walls into the blood!
What is the part?

_____

Use with page 37.

Name

Label these structures in Bert's digestive system:

throat   teeth
large intestine   tongue
small intestine   liver
salivary glands   colon
gallbladder   stomach
pancreas   esophagus

A._____
B._____
C._____
D._____
E._____
F._____
G._____
H._____
I._____
J._____
K._____
L._____

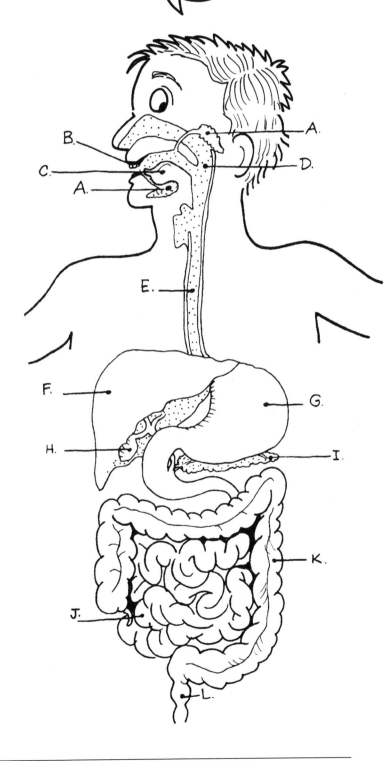

It takes approximately 24 hours for something to move all the way through the digestive system.

Use with page 36.

Name

OUT OF CONTROL

Today's patients at the clinic all have complaints that might mean one of their glands is out of control. Glands are parts of the endocrine system. They make different substances called hormones. These hormones help to control different chemicals that have jobs in the body.

The patient list describes the hormone and its function. You find the name of the gland that has a problem.

Patient	Gland Having Trouble	Hormone Produced by the Gland	The Function of That Hormone
# 1 Mr. Akum Plainer		several different hormones	controls growth; controls many other glands
# 2 Miss Swift		adrenalin	regulates metabolism and body activity in emergencies
# 3 J.J. Sweet		insulin	controls the amount of sugar in the blood and the storage of sugar in the liver
# 4 Cal Achey		parathormone	regulates calcium and phosphorus in the blood and tissues
# 5 Mel deSloe		Thyroxine	controls metabolism in the body (the rate at which the body uses its food)
# 6 Ms. L. Brainey		estrogen	controls the production of eggs; controls female characteristics
# 7 Charlie Lane		testosterone	controls the production of sperm cells; controls male characteristics

Name

PLENTY OF WASTE

The guys that collect trash around the clinic find some pretty interesting stuff. Tonight, one of them found several lists of organs that help to remove waste from the body. It's a big job to get rid of all the waste in the body. There are several organs that take part in this job. Someone was listing those organs and the kinds of waste they remove. The problem is, these lists were not quite right. That's probably why they were thrown in the trash.

Look at each list. One of the organs on each list does not belong. Find it and cross it off.

1. Removes Water From Body

kidneys
liver
ureter
urethra
bladder
skin

2. Removes Carbon Dioxide From Body

lungs
pancreas

3. Removes Body Heat

skin
large intestine
lungs

Learning about waste removal is not just a waste of time!

5. Removes Salt From Body

skin
small intestine

4. Filters Toxic Substances From Blood

kidneys
skin

6. Carries Urine To or From Bladder

ureters
urethras
spleen

8. Removes Chemical Wastes From Blood

kidneys
bladder
liver
skin

9. Removes Solid Wastes From Body

large intestine
skin

7. Stores Urine In Body

bladder
gallbladder

Name

SCREAMS & GENES

It's busy and noisy in the clinic's nursery. Fifteen new babies were born today, including two sets of twins! If it weren't for the reproductive system, this wouldn't be such a lively place.

See if you can answer these questions. They all have to do with the babies in the nursery!

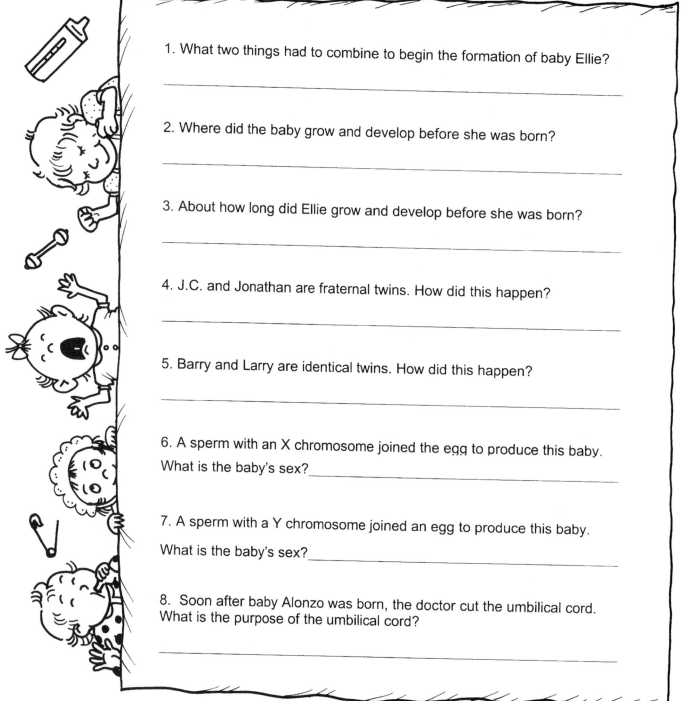

1. What two things had to combine to begin the formation of baby Ellie?

_____

2. Where did the baby grow and develop before she was born?

_____

3. About how long did Ellie grow and develop before she was born?

_____

4. J.C. and Jonathan are fraternal twins. How did this happen?

_____

5. Barry and Larry are identical twins. How did this happen?

_____

6. A sperm with an X chromosome joined the egg to produce this baby. What is the baby's sex?_____

7. A sperm with a Y chromosome joined an egg to produce this baby. What is the baby's sex?_____

8. Soon after baby Alonzo was born, the doctor cut the umbilical cord. What is the purpose of the umbilical cord?

_____

Use with page 41.

Name

9. Everybody is *ooohing* and *aahhhing* over baby Cici. Someone says she looks like Aunt Clarissa. Someone else says she inherited her curls from her dad.

What is heredity?_____

10. Grandparents are saying that baby James has good genes.

What are genes?_____

11. How did baby James get his genes?_____

BABY'S FIRST BOOK

Height: _21 inches_
Weight: _7 lb. 6oz._
Hair: _brown_
Sex: _female_
Eyes: _blue_
Other characteristics: _dimples, curly hair_

12 – 15: Circle one or more correct answers.

12. These are characteristics baby George will have when he grows up. Which of them were passed to him through his genes?

  a. the ability to tie his shoes

  b. his freckles

  c. the ability to roll his tongue

  d. the ability to make a chocolate pie

13. These are characteristics baby Lucy will have at age 10. Which of them were passed to her through her genes?

  a. her dimples

  b. her red hair

  c. her round ear lobes

  d. the ability to ride a skateboard

14. Baby Michael's mom has brown hair. His dad has blonde hair. What color hair is most likely for Michael?

  a. red

  b. blonde

  c. brown

15. Baby Will has red hair and freckles. Which is most likely?

  a. Both parents have red hair and freckles.

  b. One parent has red hair. The other parent has freckles.

  c. Neither parent has red hair or freckles.

Use with page 40.

Name _____

CALL AN AMBULANCE!

There have been an unusual number of calls to the Emergency Room today. To the operator on duty, it seems as if everyone in the city is sick or injured! All the patients want answers and attention for their diseases or ailments.

Each patient gives a description of the problem. What could the problem be? Write a possible ailment from the list next to each description.

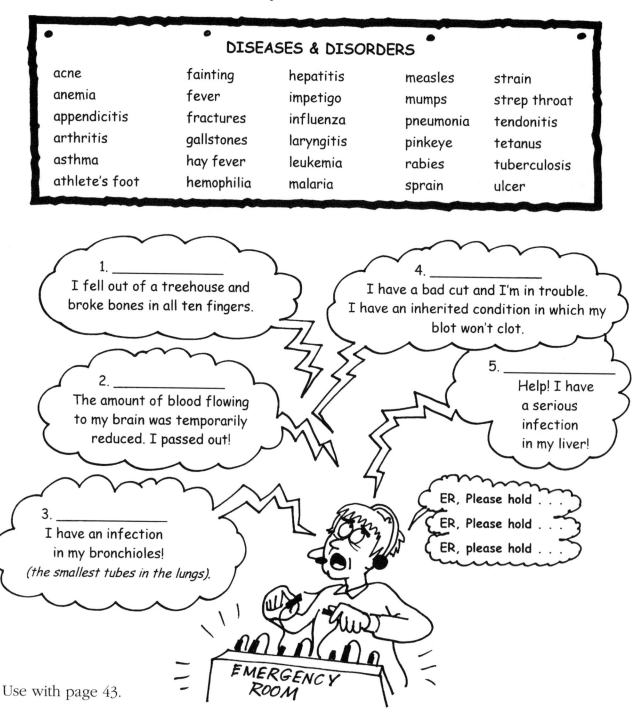

DISEASES & DISORDERS

acne	fainting	hepatitis	measles	strain
anemia	fever	impetigo	mumps	strep throat
appendicitis	fractures	influenza	pneumonia	tendonitis
arthritis	gallstones	laryngitis	pinkeye	tetanus
asthma	hay fever	leukemia	rabies	tuberculosis
athlete's foot	hemophilia	malaria	sprain	ulcer

1. _____
I fell out of a treehouse and broke bones in all ten fingers.

2. _____
The amount of blood flowing to my brain was temporarily reduced. I passed out!

3. _____
I have an infection in my bronchioles!
(the smallest tubes in the lungs).

4. _____
I have a bad cut and I'm in trouble. I have an inherited condition in which my blot won't clot.

5. _____
Help! I have a serious infection in my liver!

ER, Please hold . . .
ER, Please hold . . .
ER, please hold . . .

EMERGENCY ROOM

Use with page 43.

Name

6. _____
My white blood cells are continually increasing in number. The marrow in my bones is not working right. It keeps producing too many of these cells.

7. _____
A rash has broken out all over my body, caused by a virus.

9. _____
After a mosquito bit me, I got this infectious disease that gives me a fever and terrible chills.

8. _____
I can't breathe! I have been wheezing and struggling for air for an hour, and my bronchioles are blocked.

10. _____
The parotid glands in my neck are infected and very swollen.

11. _____
My body temperature is 5 degrees above normal.

12. _____
My eyes are itching and my nose is twitching. I can't stop sneezing.

13. _____
My joints are sore and swollen all the time.

14. _____
My appendix is so inflamed and infected that it is about to burst!

16. _____
My feet itch like mad from a yucky fungal infection.

15. _____
I hopped off a scooter and twisted my ankle joint way too far.

17. _____
I have lost my voice! My voice box is inflamed!

18. _____
There is a hole in my tooth caused by decay.

19. _____
I have an infected eyelid.

Please hold....

20. _____
A dog bit me! I'm afraid that he's given me a deadly viral disease!

Use with page 42.

Name _____

ARMED AGAINST DISEASE

There's a long line at the emergency room today. Sam Sharpe slipped on a large spider in his bathtub. Trudy McTuff's pet alligator bit her. Abigail mistakenly ate a caterpillar with her salad. Mortimer Klug fell out of a hot-air balloon. And Lucy Greene has had a fever for two weeks.

Fortunately for these patients and many others, the body has a wonderful system of natural defenses to help them fight against injuries and disease. Some of the natural defenses help prevent further problems from developing. Other body defenses help patients heal from ailments.

Give a brief description of the job each one does in helping the body heal or defend against disease.

1. white blood cells _____

   _____

2. antibodies _____

   _____

3. platelets in the blood _____

   _____

4. saliva _____

   _____

5. bone cells _____

   _____

6. fever _____

   _____

7. mucus in the nose and throat _____

   _____

8. clean, unbroken skin _____

   _____

9. acid in the stomach _____

   _____

10. reflexes (eye-blinking, sneezing, coughing) _____

   _____

Use with page 45.

Name

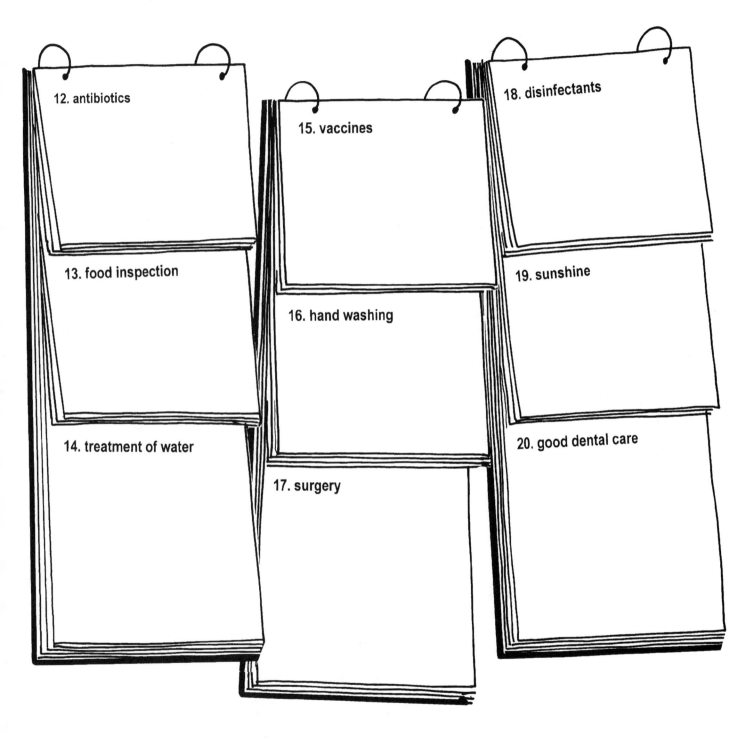

Yes! The body's defense system is amazing! But even with its natural ability to heal and fight off disease, our bodies can use all the help they can get from outside. Many diseases and injuries could be avoided before they begin!

Describe a way that each one of these help to defend against disease or the spread of disease.

12. antibiotics

13. food inspection

14. treatment of water

15. vaccines

16. hand washing

17. surgery

18. disinfectants

19. sunshine

20. good dental care

Use with page 44.

Name

SMART EATING

In the clinic's kitchen, Chef Brady Braize plans the menus for all the patients in the clinic. He also gives good advice to them about how to have healthy diets. Sometimes he writes notes to answer patients' personal questions about nutrition. Today Chef Braize went home early after slicing his thumb with his new carving knife. His assistant, Miss Plum, finished writing the notes. She got confused about some of the advice.

Read the notes carefully. Correct any errors by crossing out words and writing correct words.

#1
Note to Ms. Okra
Eat no more than 2 servings of fruits and vegetables a day.

2
Note to Andy Pasto
Make sure you eat more simple carbohydrates than complex carbohydrates.

3
Note to J. Cheddar
You should eat cream, butter, and hard cheeses in large amounts.

4
Note to Ms. Olive Oyl
Fish, turkey, canola oil, and peanut oil are good sources of saturated fat.

5
Note to J. Fizz
Foods with sugar will give you a high level of nutrients with a high level of calories.

6
Note to T. Bacon
Avoid fats that are of animal origin.

9
Note to Art Errey
What you eat cannot have any effect on your heart disease.

7
Note to Noah Lymet
The kinds of food you eat are important, but the number of calories is not.

8
Note to G. Ruff
It's a good idea to get plenty of fiber in your diet. Meat and milk are good sources of fiber.

10
Note to Bee Allance
The healthiest diet contains large amounts of only one kind of food.

Use with page 47.

Name

Chef Braize knows the importance of a balanced diet. He also knows about the values different kinds of foods have for the body. This is today's menu of all the different dishes that have been prepared in his kitchen. Use the dishes on the menu to finish the sentences below.

1. Two sources of Vitamin C are:_____

   _____

2. These are three sources of fiber:_____

   _____

3. A food that would be good for providing energy

   would be: _____

4. This food would be good for the eyesight:

   _____

5. These 3 foods will strengthen teeth and bones:

   _____

   _____

6. A source of iron would be: _____

7. These 3 foods are sources of protein:_____

   _____

8. This menu item contains protein, carbohydrates,

   and fat:_____

9. This is a source of calcium:_____

10. This might be high in fat: _____

11. This food would supply the body with

    carbohydrates:_____

12. These two choices are high in sugar:

    _____

Today's Menu

grilled salmon filets
baked lemon chicken breasts
sliced roast beef
sautéed liver strips
lentil-barley soup
cheese & bean burritos
ham & Swiss cheese sandwich
wild rice
granola with walnuts
whole wheat pancakes
macaroni & cheese
cheesy beef & rice casserole
sausage-cheese pizza
steamed spinach
steamed broccoli
fresh carrots & celery
salad & blue cheese dressing
baked sweet potatoes
mashed yellow squash
melon slices
mixed berries
prune juice
sliced apples
grapefruit & orange slices
lemon meringue pie
cottage cheese
low-fat milk
peach yogurt
chocolate pudding
biscuits with butter
strawberry milkshake
molasses cookies

Use with page 46.

Name _____

SMART EXERCISING

At the clinic's Fitness Center,
Dr. Della Toyd gives advice to
the clients about smart exercising.
What answers do you think she
will give to these questions?

1. What is cardiac output?

2. Why is it important to
   increase cardiac output?

3. How does exercise help me
   control my weight?

4. How does exercise help me
   deal with stress?

5. What should I do before
   starting vigorous aerobic
   exercise?

6. What will happen to my
   muscles if I don't exercise
   much?

7. How does bad posture affect
   my health?

8. What can happen to my
   muscles if I exercise hard,
   then stop suddenly?

1. Dr. Toyd's answer:

2. Dr. Toyd's answer:

3. Dr. Toyd's answer:

4. Dr. Toyd's answer:

5. Dr. Toyd's answer:

6. Dr. Toyd's answer:

7. Dr. Toyd's answer:

8. Dr. Toyd's answer:

Use with page 49.

Name

The program Dr. Toyd plans for each client includes the three different kinds of exercise needed by the body. She knows that a balanced program of exercise will help all the parts of the body work better.

Describe the three kinds of exercise needed.

AEROBIC EXERCISE

What is it?

How does it benefit the body?

What kinds of activities provide it?

FLEXIBILITY EXERCISE

What is it?

How does it benefit the body?

What kinds of activities provide it?

STRENGTHENING EXERCISE

What is it?

How does it benefit the body?

What kinds of activities provide it?

Use with page 48.

Name _____

SMART ACTIONS

Alex Spacey has been a student in the clinic's Safety & First Aid Class for six weeks. He has taken notes about emergencies, accidents, injuries, and other situations. He has written down the situation and the suggestions for smart actions in each situation. The trouble is . . . he did not connect the actions to the situations. He wrote them in two separate places! Poor Alex! Now that the class is over, he is trying to remember which actions fit which situation.

Help Alex out by writing at least one number from the second notebook that shows a correct action for each situation on this page. There may be more than one correct answer, and some of the actions might be right for more than one situation.

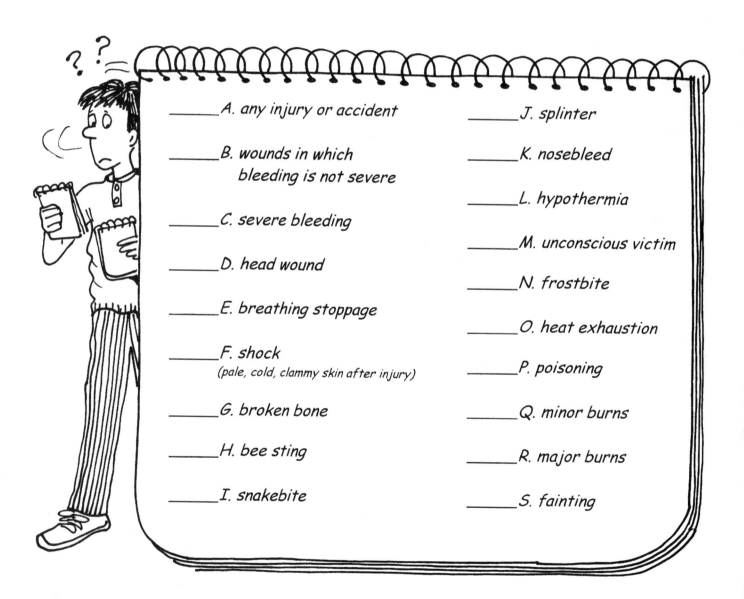

_____ A. any injury or accident

_____ B. wounds in which bleeding is not severe

_____ C. severe bleeding

_____ D. head wound

_____ E. breathing stoppage

_____ F. shock
(pale, cold, clammy skin after injury)

_____ G. broken bone

_____ H. bee sting

_____ I. snakebite

_____ J. splinter

_____ K. nosebleed

_____ L. hypothermia

_____ M. unconscious victim

_____ N. frostbite

_____ O. heat exhaustion

_____ P. poisoning

_____ Q. minor burns

_____ R. major burns

_____ S. fainting

Use with page 51.

Name

1. Get medical help immediately.
2. Wash the area with soap and water.
3. Get someone to do CPR.
4. Watch for allergic reaction.
5. Apply ice.
6. Apply direct pressure with a clean cloth over the wound.
7. Remove stinger by gently scraping it out of the skin.
8. Keep the victim quiet and still.
9. Do not touch the affected skin.
10. Do not give anything to eat or drink.
11. Do not pull the stinger out with fingernails.
12. Keep the victim warm with a warm covering.
13. Run cold water over the area.
14. Wrap the area in a blanket.
15. Remove it with a sterile needle.
16. Pinch the nostrils together.
17. Give the victim plenty of fruit juices and water.
18. Give the victim salt water.
19. Have the victim sit down and lean forward.
20. Dip the area into warm water (not hot).
21. Do not move the injured area.
22. Have the victim lower his/her head between the knees.
23. Give the victim hot fluids to drink.
24. Call the Poison Control Center.
25. Save the label from the container.
26. Give the victim milk or water to drink (if conscious).
27. Remove wet clothing from the victim.
28. Get the person to a cool, shady area.
29. Raise the victim's feet.
30. Give the victim orange juice or water with baking soda & salt.
31. Get the victim near a source of heat.
32. Examine the victim for bleeding or stoppage of breathing.
33. Don't waste time.
34. Do not move the victim.

FIRST
AID
CLASS

TEST
ON
TUE

Use with page 50.

Name

SMART CHOICES

Everyone who takes part in any of the clinic's health and fitness courses makes a personal plan for his or her own health choices. The plan starts with a list that helps each visitor check up on his or her health behaviors. After finishing the checklist, visitors set goals about better choices they want to make.

How many smart choices do you make on a regular basis? Put a checkmark next to each one you do regularly. Then set two goals for changing your choices or improving your health behavior.

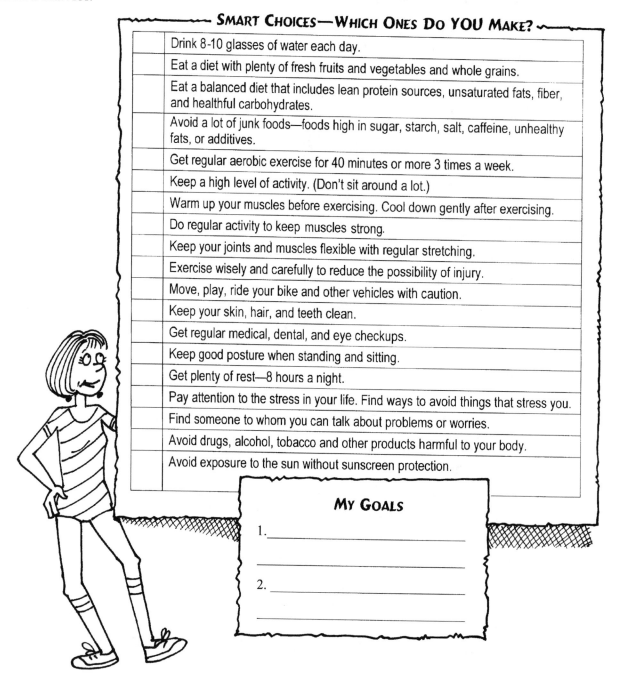

SMART CHOICES—WHICH ONES DO YOU MAKE?

	Drink 8-10 glasses of water each day.
	Eat a diet with plenty of fresh fruits and vegetables and whole grains.
	Eat a balanced diet that includes lean protein sources, unsaturated fats, fiber, and healthful carbohydrates.
	Avoid a lot of junk foods—foods high in sugar, starch, salt, caffeine, unhealthy fats, or additives.
	Get regular aerobic exercise for 40 minutes or more 3 times a week.
	Keep a high level of activity. (Don't sit around a lot.)
	Warm up your muscles before exercising. Cool down gently after exercising.
	Do regular activity to keep muscles strong.
	Keep your joints and muscles flexible with regular stretching.
	Exercise wisely and carefully to reduce the possibility of injury.
	Move, play, ride your bike and other vehicles with caution.
	Keep your skin, hair, and teeth clean.
	Get regular medical, dental, and eye checkups.
	Keep good posture when standing and sitting.
	Get plenty of rest—8 hours a night.
	Pay attention to the stress in your life. Find ways to avoid things that stress you.
	Find someone to whom you can talk about problems or worries.
	Avoid drugs, alcohol, tobacco and other products harmful to your body.
	Avoid exposure to the sun without sunscreen protection.

MY GOALS

1._____

_____

2._____

_____

Name

52

APPENDIX

CONTENTS

TERMS FOR HUMAN BODY & HEALTH

adrenalin–hormone released by adrenal glands

aerobic exercise–exercise that strengthens the heart and lungs

alveoli–air-filled sacs in the lungs

antibodies–proteins made by the body that destroy poisons created by germs

aorta–largest artery in the body; carries blood away from the heart

arteries–vessels carrying blood away from the heart

atrium–one of two upper chambers of the heart

auditory canal–tube leading from outer ear to inner ear

auditory nerve–nerve that carries sound vibrations and messages to the brain

bile–substance produced by the liver that breaks down fats

bladder–organ that stores urine

bone marrow–soft tissue at center of bone; blood cells are made here

bronchi–branch tubes in the respiratory system

bronchioles–smaller tubes into the lungs; branches off the bronchi

carbohydrates–energy-rich compound that comes from foods cartilage–rubbery protein that cushions movable joints

cardiac muscle–muscle in the heart

central nervous system–brain and spinal cord

cerebellum–part of the brain that controls balance and voluntary muscle action

cerebrum–largest part of the brain; controls thinking and awareness

cochlea–spiral-shaped ear structure; sound waves stimulate it to produce nerve impulses

colon–the last section of the large intestine

cornea–tough, protective outer covering of the eye

dermis–second layer of the skin

diaphragm–muscle between chest cavity and abdomen

epidermis–protective outer layer of skin

epiglottis–protective flap at the top of the trachea

Eustachian tubes–bony tubes that equalize pressure in the ear

gallbladder–organ that produces bile

genes–units of inheritance passed from parents to offspring

genetics–study of heredity

heredity–the passing of traits from parents to offspring

insulin–hormone that controls the amount of sugar in the bloodstream and the storage of sugar in the liver

iris–colored part of the eye; muscle that expands and contracts to let light into the eye

joints–place where a bone joins to another

kidneys–organs that remove waste from the blood

larynx–voice box

ligaments–strong, flexible fibers that hold bones together and stretch to allow bending at joints

liver–organ that cleans wastes from the blood and stores useful substances

lens–transparent disc in the eye that bends light to focus images

medulla–part of the brain at the base of the skull; controls involuntary muscle activities

neuron–a nerve cell

optic nerve–nerve that carries messages from the eyes to the brain

organ–a group of tissues that work together to perform some life activities

ovaries–female organs that produce eggs

ovum–a female reproductive cell; an egg

pancreas–organ that produces insulin which controls sugar in the blood

parathyroids–glands that regulate the balance of calcium in the bones and blood

peripheral nervous system–nerves not including those in the brain and spinal cord

pituitary–master gland of the body; produces growth hormones

plasma–fluid in which blood cells travel

platelets–substances in the blood that produce clots

proteins–organic compounds made of amino acids; important body nutrients

pulmonary arteries–vessels that carry oxygen-rich blood from the lungs

pulmonary veins–vessels that carry carbon dioxide-laden blood to the lungs

pupil–tiny opening in the eye that lets light in

receptors–nerve cells that receive impulses

retina–screen of light-sensitive receptor cells which receive images in the back of the eye

semicircular canals–canals in the ear containing fluid; help keep balance

smooth muscle–involuntary muscle present in walls of many internal organs

sperm–male reproductive cell

spinal cord–thick cord of nerves that runs from the brain through the vertebrae

stirrup, hammer, anvil–three bones of the inner ear that carry vibrations from sound to the auditory nerve

striated muscle–voluntary muscle made of bands called striations (also called skeletal muscle)

system–a group of organs that work together in the body to carry out life activities

taste buds–groups of receptor cells on the tongue sensitive to substances dissolved in saliva

tendons–strong bands of tissue that attach the ends of muscle fibers to bones

testes–sperm-producing organ of the male reproductive system

thyroid–gland that controls the rate at which food is used in the body

issue–groups of similar cells that specialize to do a particular job in the body

trachea–windpipe; tube carrying air from the mouth to the lungs

trait–a characteristic

urethra–tube that carries urine out of the bladder and out of the body

ureters–tubes that carry urine from the kidneys to the bladder

uterus–female reproductive organ which holds a growing fetus

veins–vessels that carry blood toward the heart

ventricle–one of two lower heart chambers

HUMAN BODY & HEALTH SKILLS TEST

Each correct answer is worth 1 point.
Total possible points: 60.

1–11. Which body part performs each function?
Write a letter from the list to match each description.

____ 1. attaches bones to muscles

____ 2. controls muscle activities and balance

____ 3. produces blood cells

____ 4. regulates body growth

____ 5. closes to keep food out of trachea

____ 6. focuses light within the eye

____ 7. carry blood to the heart

____ 8. contains the nerves and blood vessels of a tooth

____ 9. helps the blood clot

____10. makes antibodies to fight disease

____11. carries food from the mouth to the stomach

A. bone marrow
B. ligaments
C. arteries
D. tendons
E. white blood cells
F. cerebrum
G. pituitary gland
H. valves
I. epiglottis
J. cerebellum
K. veins
L. red blood cells
M. lens
N. pulp
O. pancreas
P. trachea
Q. platelets
R. esophagus

12–19: Write an answer for each question.

12. What body structures combine to make up a tissue?_____

13. What body structures combine to make up an organ? _____

14. What body structures combine to make up a system?_____

15. What body system produces hormones that control body functions?_____

16. What body system turns food into a form that the body can use? _____

17. What body system transports nutrients and oxygen to all the body's cells?_____

18. What kind of joint is shown?
   a. sliding joint   b. hinge joint   c. ball & socket joint   d. swivel joint

19. Name two places that this kind of joint can be found in the body.

_____

Name _____

20-23: Write the name and function of each body part pictured.

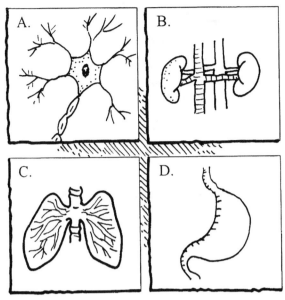

20. A. name _____

    function: _____

21. B. name _____

    function: _____

22. C. name _____

    function: _____

23. D. name _____

    function: _____

24–30 and 32: Write an answer for each question.

24. What is the purpose of ligaments? _____

25. What organs are part of the central nervous system? _____

26. What kind of tissue lines blood vessels? _____

27. What part of the eye opens and closes the pupil?_____

28. What structure sends messages from the ear to the brain?_____

29. What body structures allow you to taste? _____

30. What organ removes salt from the body? _____

31. Which bones are **not** shown here?
    (Circle one or more.)

    a. pelvis

    b. humerus

    c. femur

    d. tibia

    e. clavicle

    f. fibula

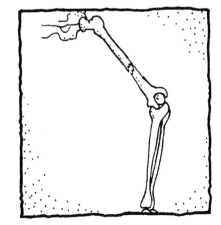

32. Which bone is broken?

_____

Name

33–40: Circle one or more correct answers.

33. Nerve endings in the skin that sense heat, cold, pressure, and pain are located in
    a. the dermis.
    b. the epidermis.
    c. the fat cells.
    d. the hair follicles.

34. _____ in red blood cells makes it possible for the cells to carry oxygen.
    a. Hemoglobin
    b. Insulin
    c. Pigment
    d. Antibodies

35. Food is absorbed into the body through the walls of the
    a. stomach.
    b. esophagus.
    c. colon.
    d. small intestine.

36. Your tongue senses bitter tastes on
    a. the front.
    b. the back.
    c. the sides.
    d. the middle.

37. When Max bends his elbow to life a weight towards his chest
    a. his quadriceps muscle is contracted.
    b. his biceps muscle is contracted.
    c. his biceps muscle is relaxed.
    d. his triceps muscle is contracted.

38. When nerve cells carry messages to each other, the messages (impulses) jump across spaces called
    a. dendrites.
    b. synapses.
    c. axons.
    d. neurons.

39. The part of the brain that controls learning, thinking, and all your senses is
    a. the medulla.
    b. the cerebellum.
    c. the cerebrum.
    d. the skull.

40. The liver helps with digestion by
    a. producing bile to break up fats.
    b. squeezing and smashing food to bits.
    c. producing insulin to dissolve food.
    d. removing water from foods.

41–47: Write a letter to show which disease or problem matches the description.

_____ 41. abnormal development of cells

_____ 42. an infection in the liver

_____ 43. fungus between the toes

_____ 44. inflammation of the voice box

_____ 45. an infection in the lungs

_____ 46. a broken arm

_____ 47. constant stiffness in joints

BODY AILMENTS

A. bruise	J. hepatitis
B. fracture	K. arthritis
C. measles	L. asthma
D. poison ivy	M. malaria
E. strep throat	N. appendicitis
F. rabies	O. athlete's foot

Name _____

48: Write an answer to each question.

Which of the three kinds of
exercise is shown here?

_____

What benefit can a person gain
from this kind of exercise?

_____

49–52: Circle the correct answer to each question.

49. Which gland controls the amount of sugar in the blood and the storage of sugar in the liver?
   a. the thyroid   b. the pituitary   c. the pancreas   d. the adrenal

50. Which of the following organs does NOT help with removing excess water from the body?
   a. ureter   c. liver   e. urethra
   b. bladder   d. kidneys   f. skin

51. Which is NOT good advice for helping someone with hypothermia?
   a. Remove wet clothing.   c. Cover him with a blanket.
   b. Give a cold drink.   d. Get her indoors.

52. To whom should you NEVER give water?
   a shock victim   c. a heat exhaustion victim
   b. an unconscious victim   d. a victim of poisoning

53–60: Write a letter from at least one of the foods that could match each description.

_____ 53. good source of calcium   _____ 57. high in protein

_____ 54. high in fat   _____ 58. will help eyesight

_____ 55. high in fiber   _____ 59. high in sugar

_____ 56. source of carbohydrates   _____ 60. good source of vitamin C

Name _____

SKILLS TEST ANSWER KEY

1. D
2. J
3. A
4. G
5. I
6. M
7. K
8. N
9. Q
10. E
11. R
12. cells
13. tissues
14. organs
15. endocrine
16. digestive
17. circulatory
18. b
19. knee, elbow, jaw
20. A. is neuron or nerve cell; transmits messages
21. B. is kidneys; removes wastes from the blood

22. C. is lungs; supply oxygen to the body and get rid of carbon dioxide
23. D. is stomach; breaks and mixes up food
24. help joints bend or hold joints together
25. brain, spinal cord
26. smooth
27. iris
28. auditory nerve
29. taste buds
30. skin or kidneys
31. b, e
32. femur
33. a
34. a
35. d
36. b
37. b
38. b
39. c

40. a
41. I
42. J
43. O
44. H
45. R
46. B
47. K
48. aerobic; strengthens heart
49. c
50. c
51. b
52. b
53. B, F, or L
54. A, B, J, L, or O
55. C, D, G, H, I, K, M, or N
56. C, D, G, H, K, M, N, O
57. A, B, E, I, or L
58. D
59. O
60. G, H, K, or N

ANSWERS TO EXERCISES

pages 10–11
1. Blood is clotting.
2. She sneezed.
3. He's yawning.
4. He has burped.
5. He's choking.
6. She's hiccuping.
7. adrenalin
8. bile
9. She's vomiting.
10. He's got dandruff.
11. She's snoring.
12. She's shivering.

pages 12–13
1. kidneys
2. Eustachian tubes
3. tendons
4. esophagus
5. arteries

6. diaphragm
7. bone marrow
8. epiglottis
9. cartilage
10. coccyx or tailbone
11. bladder
12. epidermis
13. femur
14. cornea
15. red blood cells
16. enamel

pages 14–15
A. Max
B. Rex
C. Rex
D. Lexi
E. Rex
F. Lexi, Max, and Rex
G. Lexi and Max

H. Max
I. Lexi and Rex
J. 3 and 4: muscle and nerve
K. Answers will vary.
   Check to see that student has named 6 organs.
L. Answers will vary.
   Check to see that student has named 3 systems.

pages 16–17
A. Dr. Chou
B. Dr. Bodey
C. Dr. Toyd (or Dr. Marrow)
D. Dr. Gote
E. Dr. Dryte
F. Dr Erry
G. Dr. Cleen
H. Dr. Marrow (or Dr. Toyd)
I. Dr. Muss
J. Dr. Violi

1. c
2. b
3. a
4. c
5. b
6. c
7. b
8. a
9. d
10. c
11. d
12. a
13. a
14. c
15. a

pages 18–19

A. # 6, clavicle
B. # 4, humerus
C. # 11, pelvis
D. # 14, femur
E. # 10, vertebrae
F. # 7, scapula
G. # 8, sternum
H. # 16, patella
I. # 17, fibula
J. # 9, ribs

1. marrow
2. # 5
3. # 3
4. # 15
5. # 2

page 20

Labels:
A. crown
B. root
C. enamel
D. dentin
E. pulp
1. incisors
2. canine
3. bicuspids
4. molar
5. crown
6. cavity
7. enamel
8. dentin
9. pulp
10. blood vessels

page 21

1. hinge
2. ball & socket
3. gliding
4. pivot
5. elbow
6. ankle, knee, hip
7. ligaments
8. cartilage
9. gliding

10. hinge
11. ball & socket
12. pivot

pages 22–23

1. biceps
2. triceps
3. triceps
4. biceps
5. contracting
6. stretching
7. b and c
8. a, c, and d
9. c
10. b
11. a
12. a, c, d

Bottom of page: Answers will vary on both instructions. Check to see that student has given answers that are accurate.

pages 24–25

1. cerebellum
2. cerebrum
3. cerebrum
4. medulla
5. cerebrum
6. cerebellum
7. spinal cord
8. The central nervous system is only the nerves in the brain and spinal cord. All other nerves are in the peripheral.
9. carry messages from sense organs
10. carry messages from muscles and glands
11. pass messages along within the nervous system

Labels on brain:
A. cerebrum
B. cerebellum
C. medulla
D. spinal cord
E. spinal nerves

Labels on nerve cell:
A. axon
B. ending fibers
C. dendrites
D. cell body
E. synapse
F. nucleus

pages 26–27

Clues will vary somewhat.
Across
2. largest part of the brain; controls thinking, memory, senses
4. nerve cell

7. nerves in the brain and spinal cord
8. long fiber on a nerve cell
10. an automatic body response to nerve stimulation
11. a message or stimulus passed along by nerves
12. major control center of the body
Down
1. thick cord of nerves that relays messages between the brain and the rest of the body
2. part of brain that controls muscle action and balance
3. part of brain at base of skull; controls involuntary activities
5. body nerves not included in brain or spinal cord
6. short branches on nerve cells
9. the ability to remember

page 28

Labels:
A. outer ear
B. eardrum
C. semicircular canals
D. cochlea
E. auditory nerve
F. auditory canal
G. hammer, anvil, stirrup (bones of inner ear)
1. eardrum
2. cochlea
3. outer ear
4. semicircular canals
5. auditory canal
6. hammer, anvil, stirrup
7. auditory nerve

page 29

A. cornea
B. pupil; iris
C. lens
D. retina
E. optic nerve

page 30

1. olfactory cells
2. send it to the brain
3. from fumes in the air
4. Part of the taste of something is its smell.
5. saliva
6. taste buds
7. sides (nearer the back)
8. tip
9. back
10. sides on front of tongue

page 31

1–2. dirt and germs
3. pores
4–7. heat, cold, pain, pressure

8. epidermis
9. dermis
10. brain
11. melanin
12. vitamin D

page 32

1. beating of her heart
2. side of neck, wrist
3. Her heart beat 75 times per minute.
4. closing of heart valves

Diagram
largest vein—1
right atrium—5
right ventricle—6
pulmonary arteries—3
pulmonary veins—4
left atrium—7
left ventricle—8
aorta—2

page 33

Erma has the following items correct.
These numbers should be circled:
1, 5, 6, 7, 8, 11, 12, 13, 16

page 34

1. nasal cavity
2. nose
3. throat
4. mouth
5. epiglottis
6. larynx
7. trachea
8. lungs
9. bronchi
10. bronchioles
11. alveoli
12. diaphragm

page 35

1. It goes down the throat, the trachea, into the bronchi, the bronchioles, and alveoli.
2. They expand out.
3. It moves down.
4. It closes.
5. oxygen
6. to catch dirt and germs
7. It comes back from the alveoli, through the bronchioles, bronchi, and trachea, back into the throat and out the mouth and nose
8. carbon dioxide
9. They move in.
10. It moves up.

pages 36–37

1. esophagus
2. liver
3. stomach

4. tongue
5. gallbladder
6. large intestine
7. small intestine

A. salivary glands
B. teeth
C. tongue
D. throat
E. esophagus
F. liver
G. stomach
H. gallbladder
I. pancreas
J. small intestine
K. large intestine
L. colon

page 38

1. pituitary
2. adrenals
3. pancreas
4. parathyroid
5. thyroid
6. ovary
7. testes

page 39

1. liver
2. pancreas
3. large intestine
4. skin
5. small intestine
6. spleen
7. gallbladder
8. bladder
9. skin

pages 40–41

1. sperm and egg (or ovum)
2. uterus
3. nine months
4. 2 different sperm fertilize two different eggs.
5. 1 sperm fertilized 1 egg; the egg split and 2 separate fetuses developed
6. female
7. male
8. It connects the fetus' blood supply to the mother's; transports food, oxygen, wastes between mother and fetus.
9. passing traits from parents to children
10. structures in cells that contain messages of traits
11. from his parents
12. b and c
13. a, b, and c
14. c
15. a

pages 42–43

1. fractures
2. fainting
3. pneumonia
4. hemophilia
5. hepatitis
6. leukemia
7. measles
8. asthma
9. malaria
10. mumps
11. fever
12. hay fever
13. arthritis
14. appendicitis
15. sprain
16. athlete's foot
17. laryngitis
18. cavity
19. pinkeye
20. rabies

pages 44–45

Answers will vary.
1. They surround and digest germs.
2. They attack and kill germs.
3. They form clots to stop bleeding.
4. It kills germs and bacteria in the mouth.
5. They multiply and grow to heal breaks in bone.
6. The heat slows the growth of germs. It warns of an illness.
7. It traps germs and dust to keep them from going into lungs.
8. It keeps dirt and germs from getting further into the body.
9. It kills germs.
10. They keep harmful objects out of the body organs.
11. White blood cells surround and digest the germs. They make antibodies that destroy the germs.
12. Antibiotics slow or stop the growth of bacteria.
13. Food that has germs can be thrown away before it is sold. Food inspection inspires food companies to prepare clean food.
14. Bacteria and other germs are killed before people get the water to drink.
15. Vaccines build up immunity to harmful diseases.
16. Hand washing gets rid of germs before they get inside the body.
17. Surgery can remove diseased areas or repair damaged organs.
18. Disinfectants kill germs on objects.
19. Sunshine provides vitamin D,

which helps the body use calcium for strong bones and other body functions.

20. This keeps you from developing decay or infections in teeth, gums, and mouth.

page 46

1. Cross out *no more than*; add 6–8 servings
2. Replace *simple* with *complex*, and *complex* with *simple.*
3. Replace *large amounts* with *small amounts.*
4. Change *saturated fat* to *unsaturated fat.*
5. Replace *high level of nutrients* with *low level of nutrients.*
6. This note is accurate.
7. Ending should read: *and the number of calories is also.*
8. Replace *meat and milk* with some actual sources of fiber (*such as whole grains, seeds, vegetables, or fruit*).
9. Change to *What you eat can effect on your heart disease.*
10. Replace *large* with *moderate.* Replace *only one kind of food* with *a variety of kinds of foods.*

page 47

Answers will vary somewhat.

1. Two of these: spinach, broccoli, melon, berries, grapefruit & oranges, prune juice
2. Three of these: soup, wild rice, granola with walnuts, whole wheat pancakes, any of the vegetables or fruits
3. Any of the fruits or vegetables, any of the desserts, or breads, granola, macaroni and cheese, pancakes, pizza, rice, sandwich, casserole
4. fresh carrots, spinach, omelet, milk, yogurt, cottage cheese
5. Three of these: milk, yogurt, cottage cheese, milkshake (or anything with cheese)
6. omelet, roast beef, liver
7. Three of these: soup, sandwich, pizza, salmon, chicken beef, liver, burritos, casserole
8. the burrito, the sandwich, the pizza, the casserole
9. spinach, milk, yogurt, cottage cheese, milkshake

10. blue cheese dressing, sandwich, macaroni and cheese, casserole, pizza, cottage cheese, pudding, biscuits with butter, milkshake, cookies
11. Any of the fruits or vegetables, any of the desserts, or breads, granola, macaroni and cheese, pancakes, pizza, rice, sandwich, casserole
12. cookies, pudding, milkshake, pie

pages 48–49

Answers will vary.

1. The amount of blood pumped by the heart each minute.
2. With better cardiac output, the heart doesn't have to work as hard.
3. Exercise burns calories and builds muscle which burns more calories.
4. Exercise relaxes you and gives you energy.
5. Stretch and work up to vigorous level.
6. They'll get weak and flabby. Some muscles might get too tight or too stretched. They'll get easily injured.
7. poor blood flow, not able to breathe properly, muscles get stretched or overly tightened
8. You might get sore and stiff.

Aerobic Exercise

What is it?
Exercise in which the heart works harder or beats faster for a period of time
How does it benefit?
It builds heart strength and stamina, and improves lung function.
What kinds of exercise?
Any that keep the body (especially large muscles) moving for a period of time: walking, jogging, running, swimming, rope-jumping, cross-country skiing, stair-stepping, etc.

Flexibility Exercise
What is it?
Exercise that stretches and relaxes muscles
How does it benefit?
It allows the body to stretch and bend without getting injured or sore.
What kinds of exercise?
Gentle stretches, yoga

Strengthening Exercise
What is it?
Exercise that works muscles
How does it benefit?
Increases muscle strength and endurance
What kinds of exercise?
Weightlifting, rowing, canoeing, any work or exercise that repeatedly uses upper body or lower body muscle strength

pages 50–51

Answers will vary somewhat. Make sure student has at least one of the items listed.

A. 1, 8, 32, 33
B. 2, 6
C. 1, 6, 21, 33
D. 1, 33, 34
E. 1, 3, 33, 34
F. 1, 12, 29, 30, 32, 33, 34
G. 1, 5, 33, 34, 35
H. 4, 7, 11
I. 1, 8, 33
J. 2, 15
K. 5, 8, 16
L. 1, 12, 23, 27, 31, 33
M. 1, 10, 32, 33, 34
N. 1, 8, 17, 18, 20, 23
O. 1, 17, 18, 28
P. 1, 24, 25, 26, 33
Q. 5, 13
R. 1, 9, 21, 33, 34
S. 23, 29

page 52

Answers will vary.
See that student has completed the checklist and written two relevant, reasonable goals.